THE FUNERAL BOOK

A beginner's Primer on planning a funeral, cremation, party or other post-death event. Embalming, caskets, vaults and assorted items to procure after a death.

JEFF McKASSON

DEDICATION

How does one dedicate a book about death, funerals, the cost a family will experience to create a post-death event. Be it a traditional funeral, cremation, donation to science or a natural burial…?

You start by expressing sincere sympathy to a family that has suffered the loss of a loved one. I offer that sympathy to you and eternal respect for the life lived.

You continue by letting the readers know that they are not the first to experience a death, they will not be the last. Every living soul will die.

You recognize the funeral professionals that have studied, trained, and worked every hour of the day and night to help a family navigate an emotional and trying event in their lives.

You dedicate this book to the people who raised you and taught you in the family funeral businesses.

You dedicate this book to all those curious people who want to know what happens once a person dies – and to know it before they must experience a death so that they may be better prepared and educated to make the post-death events more understandable, less intimidating and to perhaps plan a funeral, service, event or "life celebrating party" that best represents the person who has died and the life they lived.

jeffreymckasson@aol.com

CONTENTS

THE BEGINNING OF THE END

Once upon a time...a man died...and his loving family that he left behind threw a big ol' party!!!!! Don't groan, gasp or put on your shocked face. Death is not always the terrible, sad, grief-filled end of life event you have come to expect.

Every day thousands of people are born in the United States. Every day thousands of people die in the United States. It is mortality, it is natural, it has been and will always be this way – that's "life". What every death has in common with every other death is that they are each unique, different, present different effects on those left behind. No two deaths or memorial services are the same.

Death can be of natural causes, an accident or other traumatic event. Death is the process of a human being ceasing to live. The heart will stop beating, blood will stop flowing, muscles will quit working, the brain will lose consciousness, all the bodies systems and organs will shut down. The normal internal systems that help keep a person alive will now work to decompose and decay that same body. Death is the end of life for that person – it is also the beginning of a journey towards final rest and a process of a family letting go.

One death may cause numerous and diverse reactions within the family, with friends, co-workers and even health care workers that may have cared for the person prior to their death. In the same family there may be someone who has spent their last few years caring for an ill relative – their life has only one focus. After their loved one dies they may feel a tremendous sense of loss and no longer have a "job" that occupies every minute of their time and attention. They are lost in their grief.

In the same family there may be someone who loved the dying relative just as much, but watched them suffer through physical pain, mental anguish and a reduced quality of life.

They may be relieved that the suffering has ended; their loved one is at rest and at peace. They are thankful for the life lived and understand there can be dignity in death.

Two relatives of the same dying person with completely different reactions to the death – neither reaction is wrong. A person's death impacts people in many, many different ways. Pain, sorrow, thanks, relief... A funeral can be a ceremony of death or a celebration of a life well lived – the same funeral can be both.

This writing will seek to inform you about today's typical and non-traditional funeral practices in the United States. The evolving traditions are facing significant changes due in a large part to financial realities, the migration to different parts of the country of immediate families, religious beliefs, and environmental practices – the list is endless as to why activities following a death are changing.

There will be topics and subject matter presented that will upset some. Some will be intrigued and curious at newer ways to "celebrate" a life instead of mourn a "death". Some will have a true wake up moment and determine that they can plan and control their own post-life funeral service, "party" or event.

Nothing presented is meant to shock or upset your sensibilities, nothing is presented with the intention of painting a gruesome picture of post-death practices. This is offered as a beginner's reading on what occurs following a death, the options available and the path to final resting for the deceased.

An educated consumer is the best consumer – The funeral business is a business – the deceased and their families are consumers of the funeral business' services and goods. A funeral is a retail transaction for services and goods. If you will open your eyes and look at this matter objectively you will be better prepared to face the death of someone near and dear or to effectively plan for your own passing – from at least a cursory educated position. This is a beginner's trip through a death – you can learn as much about funeral practices as you need or want from much more in depth study, or you can gain some insight and a bit different perspective here that will help you when the time comes...***and the time will come***.

A Brief History of Death and Funerals…

Looking way, way back into ancient history, much of what is known about long-gone civilizations and cultures was learned from their funeral practices, how they treated their dead. From mummies, to cremations, to burial, to feeding a body to the vultures – societies have left clues about their culture and lives through the treatment of their dead.

Taking a giant leap forward to the not too distant past we will begin a short history lesson on death with the Egyptians by taking a cursory look at their pre and post-death and funeral practices. A new Pharaoh would begin his tomb immediately after he was made Pharaoh – in the case of Ramses, he had around 60 years to plan for his death and burial. The early Egyptians were trendsetters with regards to pre-planning for a funeral.

After the death a long, but well planned ritual began – it started with embalming. The ancient

Egyptians are known to have engaged and excelled in the practiced art of embalming. Embalming is the art and science of preserving a dead body.

Egyptians embalmed people, animals, birds, more people.... They embalmed a lot, and they were pretty good at it. You can go to any number of museums and see an Egyptian mummy. In many cases you can see the body under the wrappings and still make out features that will identify the person. Embalming pioneered in antiquity has made archeology an interesting field of study, and has made it simpler to research a civilization's culture, practices, religions, politics, genealogy, diets, migrations, and on & on.

The Egyptians had special priests responsible for embalming their dead. These priest cults were very secretive with their skills and embalming practices – many of their techniques have not yet been determined or understood by modern science. The Egyptian process began with much ceremony that lasted throughout the entire months-long process.

Ancient Egyptians accidentally discovered that bodies found in the desert did not decay – they merely dried out or dehydrated, but did not decay. Their curiosity of life and the after-life led them to seek the methods and manners to preserve a person for their future in the after-life. They perfected the methods and skills to embalm and now we have the fruits of their labors and skills to view – mummies.

Egyptians would remove every internal organ and the brain. These organs would be embalmed separately and placed in canopic jars that would be placed in the tomb with the embalmed body. The bodies would undergo a series of dehydration procedures that would stop all decay of the body. When the body was dried of all bodily fluids it would be wrapped in linen and placed in the first coffin. Highly decorated with burial masks, precious metals and enamels the coffin would then be placed in a stone vault. The vaults were a measure to protect the body for its trip to the afterlife, as well as to safeguard it from looters and grave robbers.

Egyptian tombs also contained the embalmed bodies of servants, animals, household furnishings, other family members, chariots and any number of useful items that could be of benefit to the dead in their afterlife. Things have certainly changed since then...

THE EMBALMING CONUNDRUM

Fast forward to today – as a society we still generally embalm our dead. The difference is that we do it for somewhat different reasons. A dead human body is embalmed for:

- Sanitation;
- Preservation;
- And a life-like appearance.

Sanitation for whom? First and foremost a properly embalmed body is safer to handle and keep for a pending funeral service. The funeral home staff will handle a body several times before it is presented for viewing by family and friends. The funeral home staff will bathe and groom a body during the embalming process. Bathing will include totally washing the remains before, during and after the embalming process.

Is all of this really necessary? Yes. There is no knowing what may be associated with the person's death that may be contagious or may cause symptoms or reactions from handling their body. Why did the person die? Viral? Infection? Disease? Perhaps a traumatic event such as an auto accident that may have left blood and body fluids on the body. There are never any clear indications on what a body may have on it that could affect the well-being and health of the people called on to handle the body.

The funeral home staff will be required to prepare and dress the body for viewing after the embalming process, and after the family has come to the funeral home to make funeral arrangements. The body will undergo a final preparation before being dressed. There may be a hairdresser involved, there may be cosmetics applied. Once the body is fully prepared and dressed, the staff will be required to actually lift the body and place it in the casket – not a very appealing visual, but a reality of how the body got into the casket. A body must be sanitary in order to be handled safely so many times by a number of people.

Preservation is exactly what the term implies – a body is embalmed in order to preserve it for the funeral service. Embalming stops the body's natural process to initiate decay and decomposition. We will address this activity in detail shortly. By halting the process that decomposes a body it will be preserved in the state it was in at the time of death. Preservation allows the funeral process to occur at a later date without worry that the body will start decaying away. Quick note here: There is no standard timeline from death to funeral to burial. Family circumstances, a place of death, traditions, and the calendar may all play a role in determining the funeral event / process timeline.

When a family views their deceased loved one after being prepared by the funeral home staff, they expect to see the person they know and love – the deceased must look like the deceased. Embalming provides for this reality - for the body to retain a life-like and recognizable appearance.

Embalming has a critical role in the traditional funeral process, but is it required by law? No - with a few exceptions. Is it necessary? No. Can a body be buried, cremated, donated to science without being embalmed? Yes, generally.

There are no state laws that demand every body be embalmed. Often times a religious preference or cultural dogma precludes a body being embalmed. In general people of the Jewish faith will bury their dead within 24 hours of death – they do not choose to embalm the body. Muslims will bury their dead before morning prayers following a death – again without the need or desire to embalm. As a general practice Christians will embalm their dead.

When would embalming be required by law? Numerous states require a body crossing state lines to be accompanied with a burial / transit permit. Health Departments are the typical issuers of such permits. States will require or prefer that a body be embalmed for reasons of sanitation as they cross into their jurisdiction - mainly to prevent disease or fear of disease.

It is often necessary to transport a body by a commercial carrier – usually by an airline. People don't just die at home or in their home town – they pass away on vacation, they die where they now live, but wish to be buried where they were from; they just die somewhere else and need to be transported back home. Airlines expect a body to be embalmed because, again it is more sanitary. The airline company employees will be required to handle the remains within the sealed shipping casket and airline-provided shipping container. The body will be on a plane filled with passengers

Embalming is not a necessity – in many cases it is an option. A great many people and families are opting for cremation or what is also termed "immediate disposal". Immediate disposal speaks to the deceased being cremated or perhaps buried as soon after death as possible. There would be no embalming. No change of clothing, no viewing, no funeral ceremony with the body present. More later...

Cremating a person's remains does not require embalming, but the cremation should occur relatively quickly after death. Both cremation and immediate disposal are post-death options that do not mandate a need to embalm a dead body.

If a person's body needs to be held for some reason, refrigeration may be an option instead of embalming. Refrigeration of a body will retard and delay the decomposition process, allowing for more time to make arrangements for the final service or event.

THE TRADITIONAL FUNERAL

Let's take a short journey from a person's death through a typical and traditional preparation of the body, embalming, funeral and burial. The timeline begins with a death. Deaths occur every minute of the day at locations ranging from home or hospital to work, war, travel, shopping, eating out, church...there is no limit to where a death can occur. One of the initial actions the family will take is to call the funeral home. 24/7/365 are the operating hours for funeral homes. When you call they will come. It is not unusual for a family member to remain with a body until the funeral home arrives – this creates a formal exchange of care or possession, an unbroken chain of caring for the body.

Some initial information will be collected by the funeral home staff:

- Who is the deceased?
- Who is the next of kin or family?

- Who will the funeral home be working with to make arrangements?
- Does the family or deceased wished to have the body embalmed or not?
- They may ask about the type of funeral – traditional, cremation, local burial…?
- A time will be scheduled for the family to go to the funeral home and make all of the actual arrangements for the person's funeral or to prepare and plan for another less traditional post-death event.

Note: some deaths are "unattended", meaning the person may have died alone of with the family not present at their end. In this case the family may not meet with or speak to the funeral director when the person's body is initially picked up.

The funeral home staff will depart the location where the body has been and return to the funeral home to begin the preparation / embalming process. If a person dies at midnight and the funeral home is called to retrieve the body, they will generally begin preparations immediately upon returning to the funeral home. The sooner a body can be prepared the better the outcome will usually be.

This is not meant to be a class on the procedures and practices associated with every aspect of embalming a person's remains. This will be an overview that explains the process in general terms of a natural death, the tools used, the timing of the process, and the physical and chemical aspects of embalming.

<u> Cautionary note: this may be a bit graphic for some ***</u>***

The embalming process on average will require an initial 2 to 3 hours of work by the embalmers. With the body still on the transport stretcher, the embalmers will don their protective clothing and equipment. This includes a full length apron, thick rubber/latex gloves, perhaps goggles or a face shield. These personal preparations by the embalmers are their safeguards from coming into contact with body fluids that may be infected, protection from typical human soils and body waste, accidental cuts or abrasions from handling the body. The embalmers are protecting themselves from any number of potential sanitation and health issues that they may or may not be fully aware of that may be associated with the person's death.

Once outfitted and kitted up the embalmers will move the body from the transport stretcher to the embalming table. The embalming table has not changed in any significant way for over a century. The basic function and purpose of the embalming table is to have a non-porous surface that will effectively channel water, bodily fluids, and embalming chemicals safely away and down the sanitary sewer drain. Embalming tables are stainless steel, porcelain, or a synthetic non-porous material that can be easily cleaned and sanitized after the embalming process has been completed and the body has been removed and placed in a casket. The table is adjustable across several planes. It can tilt from level to a heads up position to aid in the procedural actions necessary to embalm. The table can rotate to accommodate placing the body on the table or removing it from the table. The table can raise or lower to offer better access to the actual embalming points for enhanced ergonomics of the embalming process. The height of the table is important because all embalmers are not the same height, embalming procedures may be at different locations on a body, and bodies are of different sizes and shapes.

The embalming table will be made with troughs and deflectors to channel water down the table from the head towards the drain in the foot of the table. Water is flowing through a rubber hose at the head of the table during the entire process to wash away the displaced blood from the body as embalming fluids are injected. The embalming table is perhaps the most significant element or tool used by the embalmer as they ply their skills.

The embalmers are suited up, the body is on the table and now it is time to prepare / embalm the body. If there is clothing on the deceased it will be removed at this point on the time line. Clothing may be as simple as a hospital gown or may be the person's normal daily attire or work clothes – all depends on where and how they died. Hospital gowns are a simple matter to remove – street clothes not so much. The intention is to always preserve the clothing as it is – every effort is made to not cut clothing off of a body. Clothing is folded and placed in a bag to be returned to the family if at all possible. On some occasions the clothing is not salvageable and will be kept until the family offers their permission to dispose of the clothing. It may be soiled or be ruined from a traumatic death – the family just may not want the clothes back.

The embalmers are now going to take one of two actions: perform a cursory bathing of the body before they begin the embalming process, or go right into the embalming procedures.

This is a good time to define embalming: at its most basic core embalming is replacing a body's circulatory fluids (blood) with water based preservative chemicals using a mechanical pump to "push" the fluids through the body in an effort to sanitize, preserve and to offer a life like appearance of the deceased. The embalming fluid is introduced to the circulatory system by way of an artery at one of 6 typical locations on the body. These locations are both sides of the neck where the carotid artery and vein are located close to the surface of the skin within easy access for the procedure. Next are the axillary arteries – these are located under a person's arms near their armpit. And finally the femoral arteries located just inside a person's thighs at their pelvic region, where again the artery and vein are easily accessible for the procedure. The right-side carotid location is by far the most commonly used location to embalm a body. In difficult situations multiple sites may be accessed to properly and completely embalm a body. There are also situations where smaller arteries may need to be used to embalm a difficult location – such as a hand. The embalmer has been extensively trained and educated to gain the necessary skills and knows the best avenue to affect the embalming procedure.

The right-side carotid has been selected for this body. The process next involves opening an incision at the spot where surgical tools can readily access the artery and vein. Through this incision the artery and vein will be brought slightly out of the body for better access by the embalmer. A flat tool will hold these blood vessels to allow them to be readied for the procedure. Small cuts will be made in the artery and vein to allow for instruments to be inserted. Embalming fluids will be pumped into the artery and blood will be forced out and drained from the vein. The circulatory system has numerous valves and back-flow checks that will stop blood from flowing the wrong direction – this is why the artery is the entry point and the vein is the exit point for fluids.

The mechanics of pumping and draining circulatory fluids are quite simple. The embalming fluids are added to a prescribed amount of water – 2 to 3 gallons – in the mixing tank atop an electrically operated pump – the embalming machine. The embalming machine has adjustable flow and adjustable pressure to fine tune the flow of fluids into the body. Blockages in the circulatory system may prevent or slow flow; blood clots may be present that a minor increase in pressure may dislodge and allow for the necessary flow. Sclerosis in the arteries may affect the flow of fluids into the body. The fluid is introduced into the artery by means of a rubber hose attached to the machine, at the entry point of the body the hose is attached to an “arterial needle”. This needle is actually a large bent tube that is inserted into the artery through a small slit made by a scalpel. The inserted tube is tied off to keep it in the artery during the embalming process.

With fluid flowing into the artery, blood will begin to flow out of the vein. The blood flow is controlled and directed through a metal tube with an internal plunger that is inserted into the vein. The tube is fitted with a short section of rubber hose to direct the flow of discharged blood down the troughs of the embalming table. The plunger is used to pull out blood clots that may be slowing flow, but have made their way to the exit point. The plunger may also be closed to increase the internal pressure of the embalming fluid entering the body. This creates a system where the body’s own circulatory system is the avenue for the introduction of preservative chemicals and for the release and removal of normal body fluid –

blood. This part of the process will take between 30 minutes to over an hour depending on the flow achieved and the complete replacement of the blood supply throughout the entire body by means of the arteries and veins.

Once the embalming process is finished the vein and artery are tied off and the incision is sutured shut. The sutures must be tight enough to prevent any fluid leaks from the incision – a "baseball" stitch is the typical method of sewing the incision.

During the embalming process the embalmers will "set the features" of the body. This includes placing the hands in a folded/crossed position on the body's abdomen/chest, as well as setting facial features. The facial features that must be set include closing the eyes and mouth. There are just a few ways to close a body's eyes, one is to install a small contact lens shaped device that will grasp the eye lid and keep it closed. Denture power is sometimes used as is super glue. Super glue was initially formulated to close incisions, but exploded into countless other uses besides medical purposes. It is important to close the eyes securely so they do not open slowly over time as the body dehydrates from the embalming process.

Closing the mouth is a bit more involved. If a person wore dentures hopefully the dentures were with the body when it was picked up by the funeral home – if not there are appliances / devices to accommodate for missing dentures and create the appearance of the mouth with dentures installed. This appliance is rather like a sports mouth guard – it is very thin and may have small gripper-teeth that protrude to grasp the tissue inside the lips to keep the mouth shut. Often sewing the mouth closed or using a wired rivet inserted into the jaw will allow the mouth to be wired closed. Very often it is necessary to gently insert small amounts of cotton in the mouth to give it a more natural appearance. *This is a fine point* – people view a body lying on its back in a casket – you look different standing up from how you look lying down. The goal is to have the person look as close to pre-death and healthy as possible when viewed in the casket.

Arterial embalming goes only so far in preserving a body. The bodily fluids and organs in the thorax are not affected by the embalming fluids that circulate the body through its circulatory system. The internal organs – heart, stomach, lungs, kidneys, bladder, etc. must be physically penetrated, have their fluids removed by means of a suction device (an aspirator), and contact embalming fluids introduced into the cavity by means of a long hollow pointed rod called a trocar. The trocar is attached to the chemical bottle by means of a rubber hose and allows the cavity embalming fluids to gravity flow into the chest and lower cavity. The embalmer will move the trocar within the cavity to evenly disperse the chemicals. The hole made by this operation is closed with a small plastic screw called a trocar button, which seals tight in the hole to prevent any fluid leaks. Many embalmers will aspirate the body again before dressing to ensure there is no buildup of tissue gasses that may cause adverse effects after the body is dressed and placed in the casket.

Assuming the family has made the arrangement for the funeral, it is time to dress the body and place it in the casket. Clothes may be some the family brings to the funeral home – a favorite dress or suit, uniform or even sleeping clothes. The clothes may also be ones bought from the funeral home that are made explicitly for funerals. The clothing sold by a funeral home will be made in such a way as to make dressing the body easier. Funeral home clothes will include under garments, the outer garments that may be designed to be laid on the body and tied behind the neck – the arms would be place through the sleeves, but the back would usually be open. On a man the suit coat and shirt may be a single clothing item made for ease of dressing, the pants are slipped on and the dressing is complete. With ladies the process is under garments and a dress – called a shroud in the olden days.

In the event the family brings clothes with them when they make arrangements, the funeral home will dress the body with the deceased's own clothing. Under garments are always put on, and in the case of family provided clothes the process of dressing a body is a bit more involved and sometimes a bit more difficult. Ladies first – dresses are made any number of ways – zippers front or back, buttons, pull-over, jackets, blouses, etc. All the clothing brought in by the family will be used to dress the body without causing any damage to the clothing. Cutting clothing is the absolute last thing the funeral home wants to do to dress a body.

Men are dressed basically the same way – under garments, then the pants – each leg is put in a pant leg and the body is manipulated to be able to pull the pants up to the waist. Shirts are probably the most difficult piece of clothing to put on a body. The body may have become rigid following the embalming process making it difficult to manipulate joints to allow for the easy dressing of a body. One sleeve will go on – the shirt is passed beneath the body so the other sleeve can go on – then the shirt is pulled up from behind into the proper position to allow for buttoning. A tie is a tie – clip on or tied makes no difference. Funeral Directors are able to tie a tie on a body lying on its back – it often looks better than any tie the man may have tied when he was alive. A suit coat is last – it goes on in a similar fashion as the shirt – sleeve by sleeve then pulled up from the back. The coat is buttoned and the dressing is complete. Shoes are not normally part of dressing the body.

Final cosmological touches are applied after the body is dressed and once again after the body is placed in the casket. This may be when jewelry is placed on the body. Families will often bring in jewelry - wedding rings, bracelets, pins, etc. - to be put on the body – it may be removed before the casket is closed for the last time or it may remain on the body. If jewelry is to remain on the body the funeral director will typically have a family member witness the closing and sealing of the casket so there is no doubt that the jewelry is still on the body – a precautionary action.

The body is clean, embalmed, dressed and ready to be placed in the casket. This is a manual endeavor that requires 2 or 3 staff members to put their arms beneath the body, roll it close to their chests, carry it to the open casket and place it on the mattress in the casket. Sometimes it is necessary to use a mechanical body lift because of a person's size and weight.

The body is in the casket now and will be moved to a viewing room for the family to see, a place where they may meet and greet well-wishers and mourners. The casketed body will remain in this room until it is time for the funeral service. Often the room will fill with flowers and plants from friends and family. There is a registry book for guests to sign and offer notes of condolences.

These are the first few major steps in the funeral timeline, there are also activities being performed by the funeral directors in preparation for the actual funeral service. The funeral home will make contact with the pall bearers the family has selected and share with them the funeral plans. Pall bearers will be the family designated individuals that will be called on to carry the casket when necessary. The funeral director will meet with the pall bearers and explain their roles, tell them what to expect and lead them over every step as they carry the casket. The casket is usually carried from the funeral home or church to the hearse, then from the hearse to the grave side. Pall bearers can be friends, family, co-workers, and they may be hired by the funeral home for this service.

The funeral directors will be busy placing obituaries in the newspapers, retrieving death certificates from the attending physicians, ordering programs, arranging music, making cemetery arrangements, receiving and placing floral tributes, and on and on and on.... They are extremely busy people focused on delivering a flawless funeral ceremony that pays tribute to the deceased and exhibits deep respect and sympathy for the family.

It is funeral service time – in the funeral home's chapel, a church, a civic center, or grave side – the venues will vary in any number of ways. A typical traditional funeral will be a rather religious ceremony led by a minister or priest; there will be hymns and prayers, a funeral sermon, a eulogy and reading of an obituary. A funeral service will last from 20 minutes to a couple hours...it just depends.

Following the ceremony it is time to make the procession to the grave. In many places other drivers will still pull over out of respect when a funeral approaches – it is not a law except for a few locations. It shouldn't have to be a law – people should do it out of respect to another soul.

The grave side service will be much shorter – a message, a prayer, greeting of the family and the final good byes. Once the immediate area has been vacated by the family and friends the funeral home and cemetery staff will lower the casket into the grave, close the outer container and fill the grave. Funeral flowers are placed on and around the grave and the area is cleaned and available for the family to return if they wish.

This is normally a 3 to 4 day process from death to grave, but there are countless situations and events that may stretch this out to a much longer evolution.

Normal – typical – average...there is no such thing when describing funeral services. Each funeral is different, each death is different, every family and their situations and needs are different.

RIGOR MORTIS AND...

A brief discussion on the realities of rigor mortis and other post-death body anomalies. When a person dies they typically enter a state of primary flaccidity, a condition wherein all the muscles of the body relax completely. Rigor mortis begins to set in after approximately 4-6 hours after death. It is caused by chemical actions in the muscle tissues that affect the ability to bend joints and move muscles. Initial affected parts of the body are the eyelids, jaws and neck. The action of rigor mortis is also affected by a person's muscle tone, age, and physical condition. As the process advances and the body's muscles begin to tighten, the body will lose flexibility almost completely.

A healthy and strong young man will exhibit extremely rigid muscle mass once rigor mortis has fully occurred. An infant or an older, less healthy and less active person will seem to retain some level of flexibility due to the lesser amount of muscle mass. Rigor mortis is a reality of death and is nothing out of the ordinary – do not be alarmed when a person's body seems to become "stiff".

Another aspect of the seemingly stiff and set muscles may be associated with the embalming process and the chemical's effects on the human body. Embalming will destroy the proteins in a body to prevent the decay associated with the proteins consuming the remains. Destroying the body's proteins in the muscle tissue will also serve to stiffen or set a person's muscles. Both rigor mortis and set features and muscles from the embalming process are typical outcomes of preparing a body for burial or other post-death event.

What a person dies of may also determine how the body will respond to the embalming process. Disease and the drugs and chemicals used to treat disease may have differing effects on the chemicals used to embalm a body as well as the end results of the process. Medications and treatments are meant to make changes in a person in an effort to heal them – these changes can also affect them following their death.

THE OLD WILL DIE, THE YOUNG MAY DIE – INFANT DEATHS

It is always an extremely sad occasion when a newborn, infant or child dies. An old saying states one should not outlive their children, but it happens. There are any numbers of reasons a child may die and the procedures and practices are generally the same as they are with an adult death. The caskets and vaults are smaller, but the trauma is greater.

In the event of a child's death it is important for both parents to participate in the funeral planning – one parent cannot and should not take the sole responsibility of this task. It is often the case that a father will try and shield the mother from the pain of making arrangements, but this is a false reality. Both parents will feel and experience the loss and both parents need to share the planning of the post-death activities or funeral.

There have been many situations where a family has the greatest difficulties following a child's death because one parent was not involved with the process. A child's death is perhaps the worst death imaginable and must be shared between the parents. These are the most difficult to plan for and the most difficult to carry out.

NON-TRADITIONAL SERVICES

In a brief narrative we have covered the basic death to grave scenario of a rather traditional funeral. Our attention will now focus on the non-traditional funeral and other dead body disposition options.

The first non-traditional service to be discussed will be cremation. Cremation has been a practice for cultures over many millennium and regions of the world. Cremation is relatively new to the United States and not all religious faiths accept it as a funeral practice. Cremation is gaining greater acceptance for several reasons:

- Lower cost than a traditional preparation of the deceased – embalming is not necessary;
- There is no need to purchase a casket or burial vault;
- The family can arrange and conduct their own memorial service without the cost of

using a funeral home's facilities and vehicles;

- There is no need to purchase a grave space or mausoleum niche;
- If lengthy air transportation of the deceased is involved the cremains can be placed in carry-on luggage instead of buying a shipping container and paying air freight for the body to travel;
- Cremation ashes can be transported by a person's vehicle where they could not transport a casketed body;

Signs are popping up across the country advertising cremation services. These companies are often a "cremation only" enterprise. The firm will arrange to have the body picked up and delivered to the crematorium for immediate cremation. They will offer for sale a selection of urns and boxes, or may deliver the cremains to the family in a small plastic or cardboard box. These are a very frugal alternative to a traditional funeral or a cremation offered by a traditional funeral home. One such company that has been around providing this type of service for a while is the Neptune Society. Check out any firm you might want to use before you decide – do this before the death if at all possible, when the decisions can be made in a more rational state of mind.

Cremation is the most popular and most prevalent non-traditional post-death practice. Cremation is the process by which a dead body is reduced to ash and bone fragments by means of extreme heat. The cremation tort or chamber will accept the body – it is heated to between 1400F and 1800F degrees – the process takes between 2 and 2 ½ hours to evaporate the body's liquid content and reduce the reminder of the body to ash and bone fragments. The units are a double heat chamber system that also burns the first gases and smoke produced by the actions of the heat a second time to further reduce visible smoke from the action. Bones do not burn – the bones and fragments are crushed to a fine powder consistency after the ashes have cooled. Cremains (ashes and bone fragments) are collected after the procedure and will generally be delivered to the family to either bury, keep or spread.

There are definite rules on if and where cremains can be spread, please make certain you check to see if there are any restrictions for where you may want to spread someone's ashes. Quite often families will hold a ceremony for the cremains similar to a funeral. It is not necessary to have a funeral for cremated remains; many families will spread the ashes in a place of meaning to the deceased or to themselves.

When cremation is the selected method of disposal for the body there are still several options available to the family. The first steps of a traditional funeral can be taken – the body may be embalmed, a casket may be purchased or rented for the service, there may be a visitation by family and friends and there may be a traditional funeral ceremony. The ceremony is where the traditional funeral ends. There is no procession to the cemetery and no grave space need be bought unless the family intends to bury the cremains.

There are occasions where the deceased or the family may never have thought about cremation as a post-death option, but circumstances may present cremation as a necessary or humane option. Sadly, many traumatic deaths from auto and aircraft wrecks, drownings and unattended deaths may render a person's body unable to be embalmed or viewed be the family. A hard decision may be made to cremate the body against their wishes, but as a result of the reality of the cause of death. In this case the family may have every other aspect of a typical funeral from service to burial, just as they would have if the body was able to be prepared and viewed. Circumstances may cause a change to what was planned or hoped for in a post-death situation. Don't prepare for that situation, but know it does happen.

It is also an option to rent a casket for a cremation service. The deceased may or may not be in the casket – the casket simply serves as a focal point for the service – the body may have already been cremated and the ashes delivered to the family.

Some cremains are not spread or buried – they may be kept by the family. We have seen movies where Aunt Betty was in an urn on the mantle – it happens. When a family determines they want to keep the cremains, they will often purchase an urn, wooden box or other container suitable to hold the ashes. The container would be one that would not allow easy access to the contents.

A newer development is jewelry designed to hold a small amount of a person's ashes. Necklaces are most prominent, as are rings and bracelets. The jewelry allows someone to keep a bit of that person with them as they live out their lives. You can check out these items on ebay of all places.

Many paving stones for flower gardens contain the ashes of a deceased family member. The ashes are incorporated to the concrete mix as it is being prepared, then poured into a mold or shaped into a concrete piece and used for decorations in a memory garden. This is also a common practice for the cremains of pets.

Cremation provides for numerous options of what can be done with the person's remains – keep, spread, wear in jewelry, create memorial pieces, anything your imagination can conjure up.

Immediate disposal is an extension of the cremation choice. A family will not see the body again after the funeral home or cremation firm picks the body up from the hospital, nursing home, or other place of death. The body is cleaned and place in a cremation tray, typically wood or cardboard and cremated as soon as possible. The delay would only be waiting for the attending physician to sign the death certificate. It is generally not allowed to cremate a body until the death certificate is signed in the event the doctor or law enforcement wants an autopsy performed. Immediate disposal is the least expensive of all the somewhat non-traditional post-death alternatives.

One other disposition option for the dead is donation of the body for medical research, funeral education, and crime scene research. Medical schools rely on donated bodies for their labs and health education courses. When a medical school has fully realized all the use they can get from a body, it may be returned to the family for final disposal if the family so choses. Mortuary schools rely on donated bodies for their training and lab work as they prepare to enter the field of funeral service. Another option for disposal of a body is a donation to a crime research lab. These labs are located in just a few places in the USA. They will place bodies outdoors to allow forensic scientists and technicians to witness and document what happens as a body decomposes in the atmosphere, in the environment, over several season cycles and in different climates. This research aids law enforcement in solving crimes and establishing timelines when comparing these control bodies to bodies found at crime scenes. Odd as it may seem, donating a person's remains allows that person's useful life to extend beyond their death in beneficial ways to others and to society.

EXTREME NON-TRADITIONAL - THE NATURAL BURIAL

Something one would not normally expect when speaking about or planning a funeral – the natural way of post-death. There are no laws that state you must use a funeral home or funeral service to have a burial for someone – there are laws and rules for cremations. A very uncommon practice is to bury a deceased loved one without ever calling on the services of a funeral or post-death establishment. A do-it-yourself burial, as it were.

This is a bit complicated and would require you to do your research where you live – here are the basics. People die at home every day, either from a long illness, accidental, self-inflicted causes. People also die in hospitals and nursing homes every day. The dead body belongs to the family – not the hospital, not the State, not a funeral home – it belongs to the family. A family has rights that may allow them to bury their own dead.

This would be an event that required explicit and detailed planning and preparation. You would need to know where the burial will occur, is the location selected suitable for a burial? Once a person is buried somewhere other than a traditional cemetery the ground is generally considered hallowed ground and cannot be used for any other purpose. So – yes you can bury Grand-Dad out there beneath his favorite tree next to Rover; just map it out for future generations to know someone is buried there. Let's explore this post-death possibility.

You and the family have determined that you are not as close to nature as you want to be, and decide that a traditional funeral would not adhere to your natural views of the world and environment you want to pass on. You might view your life as a snippet of time on this earth just passing through – you do not want to leave any permanent mark on the planet that says you were here. What are your options?

The answer is a rather simple one – you bury your own dead much like early settlers and pioneers did for centuries. Is it rustic and primitive – not necessarily. Is it respectful and honorable – if it meets your view, beliefs and needs – then yes.

First and foremost after a person dies at home you must call local law enforcement to report the death. They will want to investigate the death to make certain it was from natural causes, they may even call the local coroner to examine the body. This is legal and proper and necessary to determine the cause of death and to issue the death certificate – the legal document that will be used to settle the deceased's estate and affairs. If the coroner determines the body must be taken for a closer examination or even an autopsy, accept that reality. Advise the coroner that when they release the body you want it returned home. If the person has been under the care of a primary or specialty physician and that physician will attest that the cause of death was what the person was being treated for and is what they actually died from, the physician may sign the death certificate. Discus this matter with the treating physician before the person dies to avoid any unwanted surprises or activities.

The spot for the grave needs to be identified if it is outside a traditional or family cemetery or grave plots. Again – the place a person is buried is forever hallowed ground. Make certain with local authorities, usually the Health Department, that what you are planning violates no laws. You may need to plat the location of the grave site so it is known and identified on the property survey for future generations to be aware of. Now the person has died, there are no law enforcement issues and you have an approved spot to bury the dead. What happens now?

Since there will be no embalming of the body the schedule of events needs to proceed rather quickly, because at the moment of death a body will begin the decaying process. Family and friends will be called on to cleanse and dress the body. You may have constructed a home-built casket or wooden box – maybe not. The body may be "laid out" for family viewing or you may go directly to a burial. In the past bodies were either laid on a large table or boards supported by saw horses. Either way there may be some sort of funeral service with passages or readings performed by a minister or family members. The grave would be dug and prepared by family and the deceased would be placed in the grave, the grave would be filled in and covered, and that would be the end of the actual process above ground with the exception of a possible grave marker.

In order to bury a loved one in the most natural state possible there are a few things that may need to be considered. Try to not bury anything that will not return to nature – dentures, pace-makers, prosthetic devices or limbs, to identify a few. You may try to eliminate as much metal as possible – belt buckles, snaps, zippers, etc. If the intention is to return the person's body to nature try to keep manmade or un-natural items out of the grave if possible.

In keeping with the natural aspects of this sort of burial the deceased and family know and expect the body to return to the earth in an ashes-to-ashes or dust-to-dust process. The earth reclaims the person's physical being and there is not a permanent mark on the planet that this person spent time passing through here on their life's journey.

This is not a practice for everyone, but it is becoming more popular with environmentally conscious people and groups. This, more than any other burial activity should be well researched and planned well in advance of a death.

A foreign twist on this practice is carried out in the mountains of Nepal. The locals will place their dead on platforms in the mountains to be consumed by vultures. They see this as a natural way to return a person's physical body back to the elements and earth. Again, leaving no permanent mark on the environment and earth that the person ever existed.

Do not be shy about calling on a local funeral home for assistance with a natural burial. The local funeral home may be helpful in transporting a body; they may be called on to hold a body for a period of time – either embalmed or refrigerated. The funeral home may help with preparing the body if family is unable to do so. Speak to the local funeral home to see if they are willing to assist you with any of the aspects associated with a natural burial – it may be a learning experience for them.

ORGAN DONATION

Serious consideration should be given prior to death about the potential to donate your or a loved one's organs. Organ donations can save or extend one or more lives if recovered immediately after death. It is possible now to identify yourself as an organ donor on your driver's license. Always make certain your family knows your wishes concerning organ donations. It may be your desire and intention, but a family member may not know and may not allow it.

One aspect of organ donations is eyes. Eyes may be "harvested" and prepared for use later on – they need not be immediately donated to a particular person or need. In this case, there are a great many embalmers that have been trained and certified to remove eyes from the deceased. Make certain your wishes and intentions are known regarding organ donations after a death.

WHAT DOES ALL THIS COST?

Dying is not an inexpensive activity. There may be significant hospital bills prior to death. The families of the deceased are often faced with travel to return home. The funeral arrangements themselves will include preparing the body, clothes, casket, flowers, service fees at the funeral home, vehicle costs, cemetery grave spaces, grave liner or vault, minister's honorarium ($$$), cards, stamps, clothes for family member to wear, food, lodging for out of town family.....this is an endless list that is unique to each family and situation.

THE FEDERAL TRADE COMMISION & FUNERALS

In 1984 the Federal Trade Commission (FTC) decided it was time to regulate the funeral industry – prices went up as they always do once the government gets involved. Simply, the FTC sought to break out all the costs of a funeral that were, up till then, combined into one price for the simple funeral and casket. The FTC required that all costs be itemized – sort of a menu system of arranging a funeral. The service fees were the same for each funeral; the caskets had different costs based on what was selected, additional actions that in the past were just part of the service offered by the funeral home were now itemized and a price was affixed to them. The cost of a funeral went up – it was as upsetting to the funeral homes as it was to families of the deceased.

This is The FTC FUNERAL RULE: *The Funeral Rule, enforced by the FTC, makes it possible for you to choose only those goods and services you want or need and to pay only for those you select, whether you are making arrangements when a death occurs or in advance. The Rule allows you to compare prices among funeral homes, and makes it possible for you to select the funeral arrangements you want at the home you use. (The Rule does not apply to third-party sellers, such as casket and monument dealers, or to cemeteries that lack an on-site funeral home.*

These are your rights under The FTC Funeral Rule:

- ***Buy only the funeral arrangements you want.*** *You have the right to buy separate goods (such as caskets) and services (such as embalming or a memorial service). You do not have to accept a package that may include items you do not want.*
- ***Get price information on the telephone.*** *Funeral directors must give you price information on the telephone if you ask for it. You don't have to give them your name, address, or telephone number first. Although they are not required to do so, many funeral homes mail their price lists, and some post them online.*
- ***Get a written, itemized price list when you visit a funeral home.*** *The funeral home must give you a General Price List (GPL) that is yours to keep. It lists all the items and*

services the home offers, and the cost of each one.

- ***See a written casket price list before you see the actual caskets.*** *Sometimes, detailed casket price information is included on the funeral home's GPL. More often, though, it's provided on a separate casket price list. Get the price information before you see the caskets, so that you can ask about lower-priced products that may not be on display.*
- ***See a written outer burial container price list.*** *Outer burial containers are not required by state law anywhere in the U.S., but many cemeteries require them to prevent the grave from caving in. If the funeral home sells containers, but doesn't list their prices on the GPL, you have the right to look at a separate container price list before you see the containers. If you don't see the lower-priced containers listed, ask about them.*
- ***Receive a written statement after you decide what you want, and before you pay.*** *It should show exactly what you are buying and the cost of each item. The funeral home*

must give you a statement listing every good and service you have selected, the price of each, and the total cost immediately after you make the arrangements.

- ***Get an explanation in the written statement from the funeral home that describes any legal cemetery or crematory requirement*** *that requires you to buy any funeral goods or services.*
- ***Use an "alternative container" instead of a casket for cremation.*** *No state or local law requires the use of a casket for cremation. A funeral home that offers cremations must tell you that alternative containers are available, and must make them available. They might be made of unfinished wood, pressed wood, fiberboard, or cardboard.*
- ***Provide the funeral home with a casket or urn you buy elsewhere.*** *The funeral provider cannot refuse to handle a casket or urn you bought online, at a local casket store, or somewhere else — or charge you a fee to do it. The funeral home cannot*

require you to be there when the casket or urn is delivered to them.

- ***Make funeral arrangements without embalming.*** *No state law requires routine embalming for every death. Some states require embalming or refrigeration if the body is not buried or cremated within a certain time; some states don't require it at all. In most cases, refrigeration is an acceptable alternative. In addition, you may choose services like direct cremation and immediate burial, which don't require any form of preservation. Many funeral homes have a policy requiring embalming if the body is to be publicly viewed, but this is not required by law in most states. Ask if the funeral home offers private family viewing without embalming. If some form of preservation is a practical necessity, ask the funeral home if refrigeration is available.*

Actual costs for a funeral service will vary by state, region and city – there is no standard cost across the country for a funeral. First, funeral homes are different – some are single location enterprises, some are multiple location operations within a single geographic area, and some are individual units in nationwide corporations.

Do not think any one ownership model will yield a lower cost of service or a lower funeral price – there is just no way to make that sort of broad blanket statement. Larger operations can take advantage of economies of scale, which is they can spread costs over larger operations and may be able to employ fewer staff or have fewer vehicles they can move from location to location depending on where they are needed for the day. Larger multi-unit firms may have a centralized embalming operation where bodies are taken to be prepared, casketed and brought to the desired funeral home for the services.

Smaller one unit funeral home operations may employ part-time staff and have a lower overhead, lower costs from being in a remote or small town. Smaller funeral homes may have other business activities and switch to funeral mode when the need arises. Their overhead may be just as high as a large funeral operation because their number of funerals per year is so low. So many variables....

The first thing to think of following a death of a family member or loved one will be the initial preparation of the body. There is a cost associated with embalming – you have the choice up front of declining embalming if the plan is to have a more non-traditional funeral. If you don't ask, the funeral home will most likely embalm the body and you just had your first expense. There is no way to estimate the cost of embalming across the country, but a good rule of thumb would be $500 or more.

CASKETS

A great question is "are caskets necessary?" Yes and no. For a traditional funeral service the casket is the single largest focal point to the ceremony because it is where the body is. For non-traditional funerals and cremations a casket is not generally a part of the equation. We will discuss traditional funerals and caskets first.

Caskets are selected by families for countless reasons. A color, an interior, a preferred metal or hardwood, cost, status – yes status. A Kia will get you from home to work every day and so will a Cadillac. You can buy yours clothes at the high-dollar boutiques or at the discount store. You can drink low priced wine or you can order the best from around the world. You can fly coach or you can fly first class. You can buy an inexpensive casket or you can shop within your normal spending habits and life style. There are low priced and high priced alternatives for everything including caskets – it is your decision to make.

Why is this casket more than that casket? The first element to a casket's cost is the labor it takes to make it. If it is a stamped-metal and welded together casket it is mostly constructed on an assembly line with skilled labor. What can raise the price of a metal casket is the material it is made of – metal thickness, type of metal: steel, stainless steel, copper or bronze. Does it seal air and water tight – not all do? Is it a solid color of paint or multiple shades and highlights? Think about a car and all the interior and exterior options you can select from – this is a rather similar decision process for a metal casket.

Metal caskets are manufactured from several components stamped from metal, then joined / welded together to create the casket shell. The metal can be anything from stamped steel to copper, bronze, stainless steel; caskets can be made in different gauges or thicknesses of steel with gauges between 20 and 16 being the most common. Metal caskets lend themselves to easily be made air and water tight when appropriate gaskets and locking mechanisms are installed during the manufacturing and production process. Protection of the dead body is a historical action made stronger by society and religion. From birth, through childhood, adulthood and through death, society seeks to protect the individual. The desire to protect does not end when a person dies. In the case of a casket the protection keeps air, water, ground insects and vermin from entering the buried casket. Metal caskets are not the least expensive choice in caskets, metal caskets can be quite expensive if certain metals and features are selected.

Now think about a hardwood casket. The wooden caskets require more skills and time to manufacture and craft than a metal casket does. Wood caskets are all unique from each other because of the uniqueness of the wood used. Wood caskets require multiple steps to finish. Wood caskets do not seal like a metal casket can. Think about buying a new bedroom set – is it real wood or particle board with a laminated wood-look. Real wood costs more and makes a very nice traditional casket.

Wood caskets are a more natural choice, a renewable material and will be much more attractive than metal. Wood caskets can be simple pine, maple, oak, walnut or cedar. They are more "hand-crafted" than metal and take longer to construct. The finishing process for wood caskets is also more time consuming and requires skilled furniture makers to complete. Wood caskets can be a wonderful choice for a person that loved nature, worked with wood or would want a more unique casket.

Another wood casket option is the historical "toe-pincher" coffin seen in so many cowboy movies. These hand crafted casket/coffins are still be made one at a time by craftsmen across the country. If you or a loved one want the "simple pine box", this is an option you may wish to explore. Plan ahead as these are not typically an in-stock item for funeral homes.

While fiberglass is not new, it is relatively new as a material for caskets. It is easily molded, it is light, and can be produced in varying shapes and designs. Fiberglass caskets can also be made to seal like metal caskets to offer protection after burial.

On the very low priced end of the casket selection are simple cloth-covered caskets. These are typically particle board or OSB with a felt or fabric covering stapled and glued to cover the shell. These are very inexpensive caskets and do not have the capability to be sealed. They are still suitable caskets for a funeral or cremation and are offered by funeral homes for those who need to be careful with their funds, or for those who have made the determination that a cloth covered casket will do the job. Casket selection is the single most profitable portion of the funeral bill for the funeral home.

All caskets have a common element – they will all have an interior made of folded, pleated, creped fabric with a large pillow and a mattress. Many casket-installed mattresses are actually adjustable for tilt of the head and feet, as well as the ability to tilt the body towards the front of the casket. One popular casket manufacturer is also a major bedding manufacturer. Another casket manufacturer is a world leader in hospital furniture and fixtures.

Caskets can be adorned with religious or fraternal symbols, sports logos, pastoral scenes and any number of exterior decorations. They come in a variety of colors with a variety of handles for which to carry them. A casket can be customized to meet the taste of nearly any person's or family's desires.

There are many reasons families will buy the "best you have" – these reasons are not always status or station in life decisions. Expensive caskets have been bought by people to ease their conscious, because a casket is cheaper than therapy, because they are satisfying the wishes of the deceased. An informed and educated consumer is in the best position when faced with making this type of buying decision – know what you are doing before you go buy a casket – don't let it be an impulse or "guilty" purchase.

Typical caskets can cost from $1,000 for a cloth covered unit to well over $20,000 for select wood and precious metal caskets. One-off hand crafted caskets can be extremely expensive. Caskets can be works of art designed for one person's personality or used to tell their story. A casket cost has no real limits.

Where can you buy a casket? Does it have to come from the funeral home? In days past the only place to buy a casket for a funeral was at the funeral home. Now there are other options. Caskets can be bought on-line, at big box retailers, casket stores and custom casket builders. A funeral home would rather you bought from them because there is a profit to be made on the sales of caskets, but with current government regulated funeral pricing the funeral home will still earn a profit from nearly every other aspect of the funeral process.

If you determine that you want to buy from a firm other than the funeral home you may have to transport the casket to the funeral home if the retailer can't. Be prepared. If you want a custom crafted casket, usually of wood, you will need to plan well in advance for the day it is needed.

Do not be intimidated by the casket buying experience – it is the purchase of an item that you need or want to perform a specific task and function during and after the funeral. It is an item, it is a choice, it is your choice. Funeral homes will offer a selection of caskets in different materials, different colors, different designs and different degrees of post-burial protection. The funeral home will either have the casket on the property or will place a call to the manufacturer and have it delivered in time for the initial viewing.

VAULTS

Burial Vaults and grave liners are the next layer of protection that encases the casket in the grave. Grave liners are not a sealed component – their sole purpose is to prevent the grave from caving in over time. Refilling sunken graves is a costly effort for cemeteries and must be constantly monitored in order to maintain the appearance of the cemetery grounds. Burial vaults will provide an additional level of protection to the casketed body. The two predominant materials for burial vaults are concrete and metal.

Concrete vaults are far and away the heaviest and most solid protection for a casketed body.

The concrete burial vault is typically lined with a synthetic plastic liner and will be sealed when the concrete top is lowered on the concrete base with the casket inside. Sealing compound in the vault lid makes a water tight seal for the entire unit.

Metal vaults function on a different principal. Metal vaults have a flat base the casket rests on and a metal cap is lowered onto the casketed remains. The dome shape of the metal vault prevents water from rising inside the grave. Take a glass and hold it upside down in a sink full of water – the water cannot rise in the glass because the air trapped in the glass won't let it. Metal vaults use trapped air to prevent water from rising in the grave and around the casket, where concrete vaults are an actual fully sealed unit that will not allow any water or creature to enter the vault.

Though not a vault that will seal and keep water out of a casket and grave, many cemeteries and funeral homes offer a simple wooden box as a grave liner for the casket to go into. The wood box prevents the soil from being placed directly on the casket, but does not seal and will not keep the grave from collapsing over time. A wooden box will actually allow water to enter the void created by the box to the point that a casket can float inside the box. It is better to forgo the use of a grave liner wooden box and place the casket directly in the grave if a vault is not purchase and used.

Concrete and metal vaults come in many models. Some metal vaults are steel, while some are copper. Concrete vaults may have a plastic-style liner or a stainless steel liner. The many models of vaults can cost from between $2500 to $25,000. Simple wood or concrete grave liners or boxes will cost between $500 to $2000. Placing a casket directly in the grave adds no cost to the funeral.

GRAVES

The typical cemetery is laid out in rows, and sections, “gardens” and “parks”. Cemetery graves or plots are typically deeded pieces of property owned by an individual or families. These grave spaces are carefully platted to ensure a person is buried in the exact location they have purchased.

A grave space is nominally a 4’ x 8’ area – this allows for either a straight casket burial or a burial with the casket inside a vault or grave liner. A grave is not always prepared and dug to allow the casket to be “6 feet under”. Most cemeteries require a minimum of 2 or 3 feet of soil over a casket or vault. An interesting note – some cemeteries allow for double-decker burials. The first spouse to die is buried deeper and the second to die is buried on top of the first burial.

Grave spaces can cost anywhere between free up to thousands of dollars. Free spaces may be in a family cemetery or church cemetery. A no cost grave may also be available to Veterans being interred (buried) in a National Cemetery operated by the Veterans Administration.

City and commercial cemeteries will sell grave spaces. The cost of these spaces will be determined by the location in the cemetery, meaning the desirability of the grave location.

Many cemeteries will also offer mausoleum spaces if an above ground internment is desired. Mausoleum niches can be quite expensive and will be priced on the location of the niche – ground level, heart level, eye level or higher…

Cemeteries will have costs beyond just the sales price of the grave. You will need to pay for the grave opening and closing, perhaps a tent, maybe a grave liner. Find out all of the costs you will be faced with at the time of a funeral when you buy a grave space.

MONUMENTS, HEADSTONES and GRAVE MARKERS

Cemeteries dot the country side of the entire United States. They are in cities, next to churches, they may be co-located with a funeral home, they may be Veterans Cemeteries. Of all the people who have lived and died in the United States the space for cemeteries is quite small. Every cemetery has different rules for what they will allow as a grave marker or "tombstone".

Newer memorial garden style cemeteries will only allow flat to the ground markers of either bronze or stone. Keeping the markers flat allows the grounds keepers to maintain the cemetery with simple mowing of the grass – there is no need to trim and weed-eat around every headstone. Older cemeteries and church cemeteries will usually allow standing grave stones and monuments. Standing monuments can range from a simple small headstone with minimal information about the deceased, where a monument can be just that – a four-sided history of the person, their life and ancestors.

Some cemeteries will have a standing maker area and another memorial garden area – the grave location will dictate what type of marker can be place there. Veteran Cemeteries will either have identical standing stones carefully lined in formation or they may have areas of flat markers.

Mausoleums are above ground crypts that accept a casket in lieu of a below the ground burial. Mausoleum access panels serve as the marker and are engraved with the dead's information. Cremated remains may be placed in a columbarium – basically a mausoleum for cremated remains. And again, the access panel of the columbarium will serve as the marker for the occupant's information.

What will a headstone, monument, grave marker cost? This is entirely up to a family as to what they wish to spend. The choices run from no marker at all – no cost, to tens of thousands of dollars for large and extravagant monuments. It is a matter of choice and preference for the deceased and the family. Take the time to visit a local monument company. They can describe the different stone options available and may even offer bronze markers as well. Again – this is a choice and something that can be bought long after the burial.

CLOTHING

Clothing for the deceased is another expense to be considered. The preferred clothing would be clothes that belonged to the deceased. You as a family are used to seeing the deceased in their clothes making the viewing less traumatic. Using a person's own clothes will cost the family nothing. If it is necessary, or a family wants to buy burial clothing from the funeral home you can expect to spend between $400 to $700 for a burial suit or dress, with all the necessary undergarments. If at all possible use the person's own clothing.

In many cases there is a family request to have a person's hairdresser or barber come to the funeral home and do the person's hair. There can be a fee for this. The funeral home may make payments like this for you and add it to your total bill as an item.

FLOWERS

Flowers can be a significant expense for the family. Many times there are large floral arrangements laid on the casket. These can be extremely expensive and cost $500 or more. An option for some is using a flag as a casket drape. Veterans are all provided an American flag – issued by the U.S. Post Office in most places – a flag draped casket signifies the deceased as a Veteran. Some faiths will utilize a religion's flag over a casket; this would have no costs to the family and can, with a quiet dignity, signify a person's religious beliefs. If it is decided to use a flag, do not plan to put flowers on top of the flag. A Veteran's American flag can be folded and placed in the casket with them if the family wants to have flowers on the casket.

Flowers are a cost friends and other family members will experience outside of the normal burial expenses. Friends, neighbors and co-workers may purchase wreaths or plants out of respect and affection for the deceased or family members they know or work with. Often times a family may request donations to a church or charity in lieu of flowers. These types of memorial donations in the name of the deceased can be put to wonderful uses, often a better use than the brief time a flower arrangement will last. Consider requesting donations to a meaningful cause as an alternative to floral tributes.

MUSIC, SCRIPTURES AND READINGS

Music, scriptures and readings have the ability to define a person at their funeral. Traditional funeral music is hymns either played on a church organ or sung by a vocalist – these can be recordings or live. Many churches have small bands and choral groups that will provide funeral music. The Church of Christ allows only acapella music – no organs, pianos or instruments. Alternative or non-traditional services can have music provided by the family – a favorite CD, several favorite songs that are relevant to the person and their life. Music has always been a key element in making funerals and services unique and personalized. Take the time before hand to pick the music you want that will shape a memory of the person's life as presented in the funeral service in the way of your choosing.

Watch a New Orleans Bourbon Street funeral procession – somber and sad at first, then all the sudden twirling umbrellas and a brass band playing "When the Saints Go Marching Home".

Music can calm or cause a celebration while still being respectful and integral to the ceremony.

The Nation was founded and is still based on a Christian-Judeo belief system, making scripture a significant part of the traditional funeral service. There have always been specific bible verses and scriptures that are the favorites of ministers when officiating at a funeral. There is great joy in seeking out and using other non-traditional verses in a funeral ceremony. Music lyrics, poems, and passages from other sources can define a person during their funeral. Be creative in selecting scriptures and verses, as well as any prayers to create a more personalized funeral experience.

Readings by non-clerics are becoming more prevalent as funerals shift away from the traditional. Reading by family and friends help tell a person's story, share how the deceased impacted someone's life, and relay what that person meant to them and others. Readings are often original works prepared just for the occasion. Who would want to speak, what would they want to say? Would it be serious or cause a smile or a laugh? Again – there are no limits on what can be presented and shared at a funeral or service.

FUNERAL HOME SERVICES AND EXPENSES

Funeral homes are also paid for the use of their facilities, their staff's salaries, the use of their very expensive and specialized vehicles and the transportation involved with a funeral. There may be a funeral service in Chicago with a burial in Des Moines – there will be fees for mileage and expenses. Funeral homes have overhead that must be paid. Overhead includes power bills, phones, cutting the grass, washing the cars, suits for the staff, secretarial staff. Funeral home overhead is the same as any other business that operates – it is the cost of just being there when you need them. A funeral home's overhead may be a line item on the funeral bill, it may not be called “overhead”, it may be called “service fees” or have some other label.

Funeral homes will lay out cash on your behalf prior to and after the funeral. The funeral home may need to order certified death certificates for your estate, insurance and business needs following a funeral. They may be asked to pay the minister or musicians (organists and singers) their gratuities for the family. The funeral home may pay a beautician or barber. Funeral homes are called on to pay many extraordinary fees and bills for a family in order to allow a funeral to occur. One major expense would be transportation of a body. If someone dies in Los Angeles and needs to be sent to Atlanta for their funeral, the funeral homes will often front the costs of picking up and preparing a body in a far off location, have the body prepared for transit, and pay for lengthy transportation on behalf of the family when a death occurs away from home.

Every business earns and expects to turn a profit or a return on their investment – funeral homes are a business and expect to earn a profit for the owners or shareholders of the firm. Profit is not a bad thing. Profits let people and businesses operate without going broke. Expect to pay a bit of profit in every item of the funeral homes billing statement.

Outside the funeral home are other significant expenses. A family may need to purchase a grave space or a mausoleum space. If you already have a grave space bought and paid for you are ahead of the situation. There are fees to be paid in the cemetery such as opening and closing the grave. There may be a fee for a grave liner. There may be fees for tents. Veterans have the option of being buried in a National Cemetery at no cost – we will get into more detail about Veteran's funeral shortly.

The costs are many; you have choices and options in what most of them will be. Understand what you are going to do when you go to make funeral arrangements and enter that experience with as much knowledge as possible; have questions you need answered by the funeral director as you make arrangements – be the educated shopper and the entire funeral experience will be much less traumatic and may be less costly.

TIME TO PAY

In many circumstances funerals are not pre-planned by the person or family needing to have one. People just do not like to plan for a death. If a person has pre-planned and perhaps pre-paid for a funeral they are way ahead of the matter. Like any other business funeral homes will provide you with goods and services, they may make payments on your behalf, they may advance payments so a funeral may be planned and occur. And like any other business the funeral home expects to be paid for their goods and services.

The bill for any service will be the things a family selects – nothing more and nothing less. If you want it or need it to have the funeral you select, plan to pay for it. You have never walked into a car dealership, picked out the car you "need", and then left without paying for it or agreeing with the dealer on how you would be paying for the car – somewhat the same with a funeral. You will either be expected to pay for the funeral when making the arrangements or you will need to enter into some sort of financial agreement with the funeral home for the funds they are due.

Business 101, Economics 101 or Funeral 101...this is a financial transaction between parties – be prepared for that. Do not pick it out if you are not able to pay for it.

Having said that, a funeral home will not usually turn anyone away that needs their services. A funeral home may be called on by the State, an institution or hospital to arrange for a person's final services. They will work with a family if there is one to plan the least expensive service possible; maybe a cemetery will donate a grave space; maybe a minister will officiate without asking for an honorarium; clothes may be donated or given by other family members. A funeral home will help you and work with you.

Funeral homes are called on occasion to provide services for indigents, the homeless, or people with no family or financial assets or ties – they will do the right thing by society and their values to offer the dead a proper ceremony and service. More than any other business, funeral homes understand and live charitable business lives.

VETERAN'S FUNERALS

When a person serves in the military they earn several very specific benefits as a result of their military service. First, make certain you take the deceased's military paperwork with you to the funeral home when you make the initial arrangements. The form to take is the DD214. The DD214 is the official record of honorable service – it is necessary to receive every military service related benefit the U.S. Government will offer you towards the funeral service and beyond. Every honorable discharged Veteran is currently entitled to a death benefit of $450.

Veterans are allowed their choice in cemetery markers or headstones – flat to the ground or a standing stone. Flat bronze markers are also an option. Markers or headstones will display the Veteran's name, their birth and death dates, and branch of the military they served in and sometimes will list awards or wars and conflicts they were Veterans of. A marker or gravestone may also carry a religious symbol personal to the Veteran.

Veterans are entitled to a U.S. Flag that can be used on the casket if the family wishes. When a Veteran dies in a Veterans Administration Hospital they are draped with a flag as their body is taken from the hospital. Many VA Hospitals have a very detailed ceremony and protocol they will follow when a Veteran passes away, some announce it over their intercom systems, some have a special honor guard that helps take the body from the hospital to the waiting funeral home hearse for transport to the funeral home. All VA Hospitals have an office of Decedent Affairs that are prepared to assist a family with the initial steps immediately following a Veteran's death.

A veteran has the right to be buried in a National Cemetery operated by the Veterans Administration; many states have Veteran's Cemeteries as well. A Veteran may request a military honor guard at their funeral if held in a private or municipal cemetery; they are standard when buried in a National Cemetery. It is also common for different Veteran Service Organizations to perform military honors at funerals – groups such as the Veterans of Foreign Wars (VFW), The American Legion, etc. Take advantage of these benefits earned through the deceased's military service. The Veteran or their family may wish to have TAPS played at the cemetery – often local high school band students will perform this service. Check with the local Veteran's groups to see who they use for their activities.

When a service member dies while on active duty the military service takes a great amount of responsibility for the deceased and the funeral planning and service. When a service member dies the military makes an immediate notification to the next of kin as listed on the service member's personnel file – a spouse, parents, sibling, children... A military escort is assigned and tasked with accompanying the body from the place of death to the service member's home. The escort will serve as a liaison between the family and the military. The escort will aid the funeral home with any military responsible arrangements for the funeral service – these might include coordinating an honor guard, helping with the cemetery arrangements, providing the service member's uniform to dress the body with. The escort will also assist the family apply for specific death and survivor benefits. The military is extremely involved and engaged when they are called on to bury one of their own. The military escort may not have known the service member, but that is of no consequence when they are detailed to this solemn and honorable duty.

If you are wishing to have a military influenced funeral it is best to plan ahead and find out what is available as options to you in your city or area. What choices you have in Veterans Cemeteries. Plan ahead in order to have the funeral you want to have, and in the event of a military Veteran – the service you have earned.

A quick tale: several years ago a U. S. Navy Captain died in the states. He wanted his cremains spread at sea from the first U.S. Warship leaving Bremerhaven, Germany. A U.S. Navy fast-attack nuclear submarine pulled into Bremerhaven harbor to resupply and enjoy a brief port call before returning to life under the sea. The Captain's cremated remains were sent to an officer that was flying to Germany to join the submarine's crew – the cremains of the late Captain were delivered to the submarine. The submarine departed Bremerhaven and headed out to the North Sea and turned south to transit the English Channel. The weather was rough, the seas were high, and there was a tremendous amount of surface ship traffic in the sea. The submarine was making a surface transit, which meant there were always at least two crew members on lookout in the submarine's sail. The time came for the "burial" at sea – there are very detailed guidelines and ceremonies involved with a burial at sea. The ship's company was called to attention over the ship's intercom system, the sub came to all-stop, and the container holding the ashes was opened. As a young officer (raised in his family's funeral homes) was pouring the ashes over the side, the strong wind blew the ashes towards the lookout in the back hatch of the sail. Coughing, the lookout was covered in rain and ash over his yellow rain slicker suit. The look on his face was somewhere between terror and *what's next*? A large wave broke over the bow of the submarine and washed up and over the sail completely drenching the lookout and two officers in the sail – the ashes were in the sea. Mission accomplished.

SOCIAL SECURITY

As a working member of society you have contributed to your Social Security account your entire working life. Social Security will not pay for a funeral. The death benefit you have earned for your labors over a lifetime from Social Security is currently $255. The funeral home will submit the paperwork for you once they have received the certified death certificates. Survivor's death benefits are a whole other book and cannot be addressed in this basic format. Just know that there is a small benefit available from Social Security to help with funeral expenses and perhaps many other spouse and children's "survivor" benefits available to other family members.

INSURANCE

Most people have life insurance, which is actually death insurance. It is only payable when a person dies. Insurance is often the way most funerals are paid for, but collecting on an insurance policy is a detailed process. The one thing necessary to collect on a deceased person’s insurance policy is a certified copy of the death certificate. The certified copies will have a raised seal from the issuing authority – health department or other government entity.

This is also the process used to collect other death benefits and may be the method used to notify creditors and others of a person’s death. This may activate credit life policies on mortgages or auto loans. Be aware of all outstanding payment requirements a person has when they die and be prepared to settle or close these accounts or activities as necessary.

THE WILL

Everyone that works, or has a home, spouse, children or property should have a will. A will is a simple document that details your post-death wishes for your worldly possessions. A will is a legal instrument that is typically executed and recorded to allow it to be retrieved and used by the courts if necessary to settle and distribute the assets of a person's estate. This is not a book on wills – just be aware of them and determine if and how a will would benefit those you leave behind after your death.

If a person has a sizeable asset portfolio and property and they die without a will, the State may step in and settle the estate – this may not be to the liking of family or the deceased. Dying without a will is a bad scenario if you have a valuable estate or if you have specific wishes for where you want your possessions and assets to go.

NOW FOR SOMETHINGS COMPLETELY DIFFERENT

Culture and societal norms have been changing, the "traditional" funeral is being rapidly replaced with personalized events and ceremonies that celebrate a life rather than mourn a death. These events can occur with a deceased's body or ashes present or not. These events can be planned outside the normal church, religious and funeral home bounds. One example is an evening gathering with a dinner or food, drinks and stories – you might call this a "wake". The deceased may be there in a cremation urn on a table surrounded with pictures and flowers while family and friends share and recall the stories of a life lived and enjoyed. The mood is much less somber; the event is much more casual and may serve as a better reflection of the person's life than a traditional funeral ceremony in a church or funeral home. Don't be afraid or hesitant to discuss this option with your family if you are not a fan of having a traditional funeral – throw your last big party!

We have taken the spreading of a person's ashes to new heights. Rumor has it that the world renowned astronomer Carl Sagan's ashes were blasted into outer space. There are companies now that will accept a small amount of a person's ashes and send them to space. People are renting small aircraft and spreading ashes over farmland, forests, lakes and at sea. People are no longer limited to the norms of society and are seeking exciting and unique ways to honor a life. Put imagination and thought to work on ways to make yours or a family members post-death experience special and memorable in a positive way.

The SEA - It is still possible to have a burial at sea for a person's body – not just their ashes. You will need to search out a firm that will accommodate your wishes and you will be required to adhere to the environmental laws associated with putting something (a human body) in the ocean. It is best to not embalm the body and not place it in a casket. A simple shroud or wrappings on an un-embalmed body will quickly be consumed by nature in an ashes-to-ashes dust-to-dust manner, albeit under the sea.

The DAY - Unless it is important – do not plan to have a funeral on a holiday, someone's birthday or other special day. That special date will forever be the day we buried Grandpa – not Christmas or Sue's birthday or the 4th of July or Valentine's Day.... Be cautions with the day and date of a funeral.

PICTURES - Past practices and norms precluded taking pictures at the funeral home, during the funeral or at the cemetery. Don't hold back. Everyone carries a camera on their phone now – we are a visual society – take your pictures. A funeral or service is a social event that many people want to remember with pictures. The people unable to travel or attend will only experience the event through photographs if they are available. Be respectful of those grieving and don't try to stage clever shots around an open casket. It is alright to photograph the event and help to remember what may be lost in your grief and activity during the event.

A trip to the cemetery used to be a pretty simple endeavor – put the casket in the hearse, everyone get in their cars and drive to the cemetery. The cemetery trip has taken a detour in many of today's services. The route may go past a homestead or family farm, past a business or school, the route may not be the shortest. If it is important to create an alternate drive to the cemetery – do it.

Another options is to forego the hearse altogether and carry the casket another way. One funeral recently had the casket on a flat-bed semi-truck trailer being escorted by friends and family on motorcycles. Caskets have been carried on firetrucks and favorite personal vehicles. Some cemeteries still offer horse drawn carriages. Think ahead and make plans to have the service you want.

SAME SEX COUPLES - Brief discussion on a current topic – same sex couples and funeral planning. The law recognizes the next of kin as being responsible for making funeral arrangements – this may be a spouse, a child, a sibling, a parent... A person may have pre-planned their entire post-death event, but know the funeral can be changed by the person making the actual final arrangements. Make certain you are fully aware of the local laws that may govern a significant other's rights and/or responsibilities to make funeral plans for their loved one. Speak with the family members if possible before a death to gain their agreement and acceptance of the funeral plans being made. Make your wishes well know, pay ahead if you can and take as much off the table for others to change as possible. Be mindful that funeral wishes detailed in a will may not be read until well after a death and funeral have occurred. Do your homework, prepare and plan to ensure that this experience is what you want. Make certain others are fully aware of your wishes and plans, and gain their agreement and acceptance well in advance.

THE PROLOGUE

Once upon a time...a man died.... It happens every minute of every day. Educate yourself and those closest to you about what is expected, what is required and what is possible for creating the post-death funeral, service, celebration or event that best exemplifies your's or the person's life being memorialized.

Stick with tradition or craft a unique experience – just make it yours and plan – plan – plan ahead. Your life does not vanish from people's memories after you die, the post-death ceremony should serve to create lasting memories of a life well and happily lived. Give those who will mourn your passing a worthwhile memory and one heck of a send-off if that is your style and desire.

Plan...plan...plan... Death is an emotional experience for those left behind – it has always been that way and it will always remain that way. The absolute best way to experience a person's death is to plan for it before it occurs so your attention can be on the event rather than trying to plan the event. Pre-planning may allow for the deceased to participate in the arrangements and details they want others to experience when remembering their life and death. Participating in making funeral arrangements may even make the end of life an easier journey for the deceased and family if they already know the plans for the post-death activities are pretty well set. Learning and planning for a funeral or any type of service will allow you to be a much better consumer and shopper. You will not be carried away with the options and costs that you would otherwise just accept. Know your options, know your fiscal limits, know your goals towards providing yourself or a family member with the post-death service, funeral or celebration they deserve and want.

There will always be funeral homes and funeral directors to assist you with planning any event you may wish to craft, be it a traditional funeral and burial, a cremation, a donation to science. Educate yourself, learn what you need to know to control and direct the services you want, plan it, and wait for the big day...it will come.

The purpose of this book is to let you know that you will be faced with death, a family member's, dear friends, co-worker's or your own. The vast number of options available for you to select from to make the post-death experience unique to you is a major focus on this book. There is no intention to shock or dismay you with the reading – hopefully you have been educated, enlightened and entertained to some extent.

We all die – it is how we plan for it and experience it that makes it our death. Live well and live long, don't fear what you know you cannot change.

IMPORTANT DOCUMENTS AS YOU PLAN FOR POST-LIFE

Use this list as a guideline in accumulating the necessary and important documents and information your family will require in order to complete funeral arrangements. These documents would be used for preparing and writing death announcements and obituaries, applying for and collecting death benefits, closing accounts – credit and investment.

Information regarding employment and specific people to call in the event of death; contacts for legal and business matters and the location of property deeds and other documents. Car titles, bank accounts, and mortgage information will need to be addressed. These are all important items and information that someone will need to have before and after the funeral has occurred.

THE LIST

- Gather every bit of personal information you have to include:
    - Full legal name
    - Any other names you may have used
    - Social Security number
    - Date and place of birth
    - Ethnic or cultural background and heritage
    - Your Father's full name
    - Your Mother's maiden name
    - Marital status (divorce documents if necessary)
    - Your spouse's or significant other's full name
    - Wedding information – place and date
    - List of all children by full name, date and place of birth
    - Who preceded you in death (family)?
    - Who are you survived by (family)?
    - Military separation papers (DD214)

    - Education – high school, trade school, college, etc.
    - Driver’s License state and number
    - Passport information
    - Residency information if not native born to the USA
- Contact information to include:
    - Immediate next of kin – person who would make final arrangements
    - Family to be called
    - Executor, lawyer or estate administrator
    - Financial planner and/or stockbroker
    - Insurance agent
    - Banker
    - Doctors(s)
    - Employer - Provide employment dates and history of current and past positions
    - Any labor organization
    - Landlord or mortgage holder

    - Any volunteer organization, fraternal or social memberships
    - Military organizations
- Gather important documents:
    - Will
    - Birth certificate
    - Military discharge document – DD214
    - All insurance policies
    - Marriage license
    - Deeds
    - Titles
    - Adoption papers
    - Divorce documents
- Gather all important account numbers:
    - Bank and savings account numbers and points of contact
    - Retirement account numbers and points of contact
    - Insurance policy numbers and a company point of contact
    - All mortgage and/or loan numbers and points of contact

- Credit card account numbers and contact information
- Safe deposit box(s) where and number and key location
- Certificates of deposit or money market accounts
- IRAs and retirement plan account numbers and points of contact
- Internet accounts, user names, logins and passwords

Use the list above as a basis to creating your own data bank of all your pertinent information that will be needed by someone to manage your estate and to make funeral arrangements after your death. If you find yourself pre-planning for a death you will have adequate time to gather and assimilate all of this information. If you wait until after a death has occurred you may not be able to compile every necessary document, account number, or bit of personal information that will make the entire process less traumatic.

As always – plan, plan, plan ahead – please.

WHAT SORT OF POST-DEATH EVENT DO I WISH FOR MYSELF?

Here is where you get to put pen (or ink jet) to paper and let the world know what you would like for a final affair among your living family and friends. Put thought into this effort – there will only be one performance or event.

- Who gets notified and who is told to stay away?
- Have you pre-planned a service? Where and with whom?
- Who will be responsible to see that your wishes and final arrangements are carried out in accordance with your pre-death funeral planning?
- Do you want to be embalmed?
- What kind of casket do you want?
- What kind of vault do you want?
- Do you want a traditional funeral?
- Cremation?
- Donating to science?
- Natural burial?

- Burial at sea?
- Do you have any special music, songs, prayers, readings or scriptures you want read at your services?
- Do you want any military honors if earned?
- Special flowers or perhaps donation to a charity in lieu of flowers?
- Where might you want to be buried? Has a grave space been bought or reserved?
- If you are cremated, where do the ashes / cremains go after the cremation? Buried, spread, retained?
- Are you willing to be an organ donor?
- Do I want to be viewed by family and friends after I die?
- Any special clothing, glasses, jewelry to be place on me?
- Is there anything special to be placed in my casket? Book, photos, cane, toy....?
- Is there anything to be placed in the casket or cremation tray with me?

- Would there be anything to place inside my cremation urn with me following cremation? Pet's ashes, tokens, photos….?
- Do you want a headstone or grave marker? Have you already bought one?
- Do you want an alternate celebration of life instead of a funeral?
- Where, what, who would be invited to an alternative celebration event?

Get as detailed as you wish when you plan your post-death funeral, services or event. No one could ever imagine a service exactly like the one you would plan and seek for yourself. And as always – plan – plan – plan.

Once upon a time a man died…he left three numbered envelopes to be opened after his passing. His widow opened the first envelope – it contained $10,000 in cash with a note that said buy the best casket you can get for $10,000. The widow bought a $10,000 casket. She opened the second envelope – it too contained $10,000 with a note that asked her to buy the best burial vault available for $10,000. The widow bought a $10,000 burial vault. The final envelope also had $10,000 cash in it with a note that said to buy the best stone possible for $10,000. The widow bought a $10,000 diamond..... plan – plan – plan...

About the author

Born in rural Iowa to a funeral director and bookkeeper, life started out on the other side of weird. Home was upstairs over the funeral home – toys were kept in the casket display room – the first scar was from running into the corner of a casket at age 3. Things went crazy from there. Jeff finished high school at age 16 and headed for the warmer climes of Mississippi for college – earning a BBA in Management from Delta State University while working in the family funeral home in Greenville, MS. After graduation the NAVY made a siren's call and off to Officer Candidate School, followed by Submarine Officer School. Tours included a fast-attack nuclear submarine the USS BLUEFISH (SSN675), an F-14 fighter squadron the Red Rippers VF-11, Marine Corps Air Station (MCAS) Cherry Point, NC. The wildest tour was at the United States Embassy – Kuwait working with the Kuwait Air Force who flew US NAVY provided aircraft. Mac endured the Iran-Iraq war that ended in 1988 and the Iraqi invasion of Kuwait in 1990. He served with the Naval Special Warfare Development Group during Desert Storm & Desert Shield. He is a decorated and disabled service connected combat Veteran.

Following military service he worked in Saudi Arabia and other locations throughout the Middle East as a civilian contractor, finally returning to the States for good in 2000. He is a self-trained construction expert and has developed and constructed commercial projects across the entire Eastern USA and the Middle East.

The Bride and Mac reside in Texas near the town The Bride was born in – a small town near Ft. Hood. He works for the Veterans Health Administration providing his best efforts to support fellow Veterans and the civilian staff that provides them the best care in the world in return for their service to the Nation. He builds and rides single-speed bicycles. Enjoys NASCAR, golf, his boat, motorcycle and camper.

His Bride Patty is his life, they have one daughter and 5 sons between them. Grandchild count stands at 7 – one grandson and 6 granddaughters. Mother and sister (and family) reside in Spring, Texas.

****

Life is a lot like fun…only different.

CPSIA information can be obtained
at www.ICGtesting.com
Printed in the USA
BVHW040548030321
601578BV00027B/642